# Gingerbread Castles to the Max

## Written and Photographed

## by

## Ian Murray

# I. Introduction and history

All you really need to make a gingerbread castle is the right kind of dough, the right kind of paste, some candy, and some creativity. This book will tell you how to make a gingerbread castle like our family has been doing for 10 years. We build it on Thanksgiving weekend and then we decorate it the following weekend. Here is the scoop.

*Me and my dad making icing paste together. (Photo by my mom)*

# II. Starting off

T he first thing you need to do is get a design for your castle. Take out a piece of paper and a pencil and draw out what you want your castle to look like. One thing that you could do is look at pictures of castles in Europe. This year we modeled ours after mad King Ludwig's castle, Neuschwanstein. But if you are new at this, I recommend that you start small. Then when you get the design just the way you like it, you are ready to get the candy and the other ingredients.

*I took this picture to show all the candy and the drawings for our gingerbread castle this year.*

# III. Ingredients for the gingerbread

**Y**ou can't just use any dough, you know. You have to use a strong kind. The ones that you get out of cookbooks may taste good but they are too soft.

Here's the ingredients and recipe that we use:

### Gingerbread Dough

1 1/2 cups heavy cream
2 1/2 cups brown sugar
1 1/4 cups molasses
1 tablespoon powdered ginger
    1 tablespoon grated
lemon rind
2 tablespoons baking soda
9 cups flour (this causes a
    mess in the kitchen)

*This picture that I took shows most of the ingredients for the gingerbread.*

## Mixing Instructions for Gingerbread

*Whip the cream first until it begins to thicken. Add sugar, molasses, ginger, lemon rind, and baking soda. Beat 10 minutes. Add the flour and mush it together with your hands. After doing this, put the dough in a large plastic bag and refrigerate overnight.*

*This is my brother, Jonathan, mushing together one batch with his hands. For an average castle, you probably need 2 batches. For the castle we made this year, we had to make 4 batches.*

# IV. Creating walls of various sizes

**N**ow that you have the dough, it is time to start making the walls. Roll it out on a greased 11 inch by 17 inch cookie sheet and roll it to a thickness of 1/4 inch to 1/8 inch. We make a model out of thin carboard first and then we flour the cardboard, put it on top of the rolled out gingerbread, and cut around the cardboard model. Take out the excess dough and save it in the bag for the next wall. Make sure the oven is preheated to 300 degrees and put the gingerbread in for 20 minutes. When you take it out of the oven, let it cool on cookie sheets for 5-10 minutes. I suggest that you have more than one cookie sheet. We use four so that we can bake two sheets at a time while we are preparing the other two sheets.

*My mom took this photo of me and my dad making walls.*

# V. The paste

J ust like the gingerbread, you need a special kind of icing because the kind you buy at the store won't hold up gingerbread walls.  This is the recipe:

### Paste Icing

*2 pounds of confectioner's (powdered) sugar*
*6 egg whites*
*1 teaspoon cream of tartar*

*I took this photo of my dad and my brother making a batch of icing.*

## Mixing instructions for Paste Icing

*Put the 6 egg whites and the cream of tartar in a large bowl and whip at high speed for about a minute. Reduce the speed to medium and start adding the confectioner's sugar. Do this slowly or else you will look like the Abominable Snowman!! After all the sugar is in, beat at medium speed for 7-10 minutes until the icing is very thick.*

*Here is my brother making another batch. You will probably have to make four batches for building and decorating. But only make one batch at a time and use it immediately because it will harden quickly.*

# VI. Building

Y ou will need at least two people for this part. Before building, you have to get some foam core board. Cover the foam core board with aluminum foil and put it on a large table. Every year, we go out and buy alot of small rice cakes (about 2 inches across) to use for supports. I also suggest that you have some soup cans to hold up the walls while the icing is drying. Now decide where you are going to put the walls and glue a rice cake with the icing on the base at each corner. After doing so, paste together rice cakes, one on top of the other, to the height of the walls. Now, get the walls and put them up against the rice cakes and glue them together with icing. If the walls don't hold up, put soup cans on each side of the walls until the icing dries. If you want windows on the sides, before building, read the windows section.

*I took this photo to show the rice cakes that we used as braces in the corners.*

# VII. Windows

Y ou can make windows that light up and look really cool. To do this, you will first need to cut a hole in the bottom of the foam core board in the middle of the castle floor. It is best to do this before building the castle. For a small castle, insert a fixture the size of a night light. It is a good idea to leave a small hole for ventilation near the top of the castle, because if it gets too hot, the windows will melt.

T here are two ways to make windows. The first method makes "stained" glass windows of any shape and these must be cooked. The second method makes small rectangular windows and does not require cooking. For both types of windows, we find that Jolly Ranchers work well.

*The windows look cool lit up at night.*

# a. Stained glass windows

The first thing you need to do is to make a hole in the gingerbread wall where you want the window. You can do this by cutting a hole in the dough before you bake the wall. Or you can bake a solid wall and then cut a hole with a sharp knife after the baked wall has cooled.

*As you can see, we cut out a circular hole for a stained glass window.*

T hen with your hands, mold a frame for the window out of gingerbread dough. Put it on a greased cookie sheet. Now get four different colors of Jolly Ranchers and crush them up separately in plastic bags using a hammer. Then, pour the crushed candy into the mold. I recommend that you don't mix the colors together or they will make a yucky brown. Now bake for 20 minutes. Let the window cool for a few minutes and take it off the cookie sheet with a spatula.

*These are two stained glass windows we made for our castle this year. We also used this method to make a castle door.*

N ow you can paste the window over the hole you left in the gingerbread wall. I recommend that you paste the windows on after the walls are built because the windows break easily. We use toothpicks to hold up the windows while the icing is drying.

*This picture shows a window after it was pasted on and decorated.*

# b. Small rectangular windows

I n this year's castle, we put little windows on the sides made out of individual Jolly Ranchers. Get out an already-baked wall and lay it down on a counter. Take an X-acto knife and cut little tiny rectangles so the Jolly Ranchers have a tight fit. Make sure you do this before you build.

*My brother and my dad putting in the small windows made of Jolly Ranchers.*

# VIII. Details

## a. Courtyards

T he things that I am about to describe are all optional. You can make a courtyard by putting up miniature walls in a pentagon or other shape in front of the castle. The thing that we did with our courtyard was that we used the same rice cake supports in the corners and we put a walkway around the top of the wall resting on the supports.

## b. Square towers with turrets

S quare towers are made out of four strips of gingerbread pasted together with icing in a small square. Make sure that you build them around a tower of rice cakes. Then you put a gingerbread top on it. Now to do the turrets. Our turrets are actually sugar cubes pasted on top of the towers.

## c. Ice cream cone towers

I ce cream cone towers are usually used to help hold the roof up. These towers are the simplest of all because all you have to do is glue together ice cream cones stacked one on top of the other. Make sure they are glued up against the wall of the castle or the towers won't stay up.

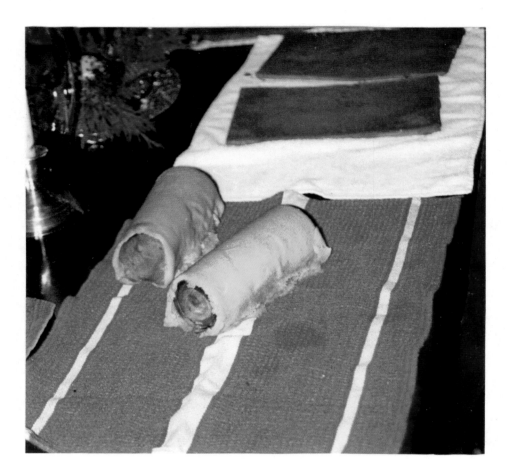

*These are the round towers that we baked around iced tea glasses.*

## d. Round towers

We build our round towers by wrapping rolled out gingerbread dough around iced tea glasses. When they are done baking, let them cool and then carefully slide the glasses out.

## e. Gargoyles

A gargoyle is a little mutant creature usually used to decorate castles and cathedrals in Europe. We hand molded little faces using our clay modeling skills. Bake for about 15 minutes. Let them cool and paste them where you like.

*I made the two gargoyles on the left and my brother made the two on the right.*

# f. Pretzel gates and other ideas

For the gate, we molded a gingerbread frame and then pressed in pretzel sticks and baked it for 15-20 minutes. We also used this method to make a ventilation window at the back of the castle. To make a drawbridge, we pasted together pretzel rods and pretzel sticks. We also hand molded some columns to paste next to the gates.

*Pretzel sticks can be used to make gates or windows with bars.*

# IX. The Roof

**R**oll out two slabs of gingerbread for a pitched roof and cut out notches to go around the towers which will help hold up the roof. Then you cook them for 25 minutes so that they are really hard. Let them cool and then you paste them on with icing. Let the castle sit overnight so that it dries before decorating.

# X. Decorating

**D**ecorating usually takes two days to accomplish. Make sure you have a big variety of candy so your castle looks colorful.

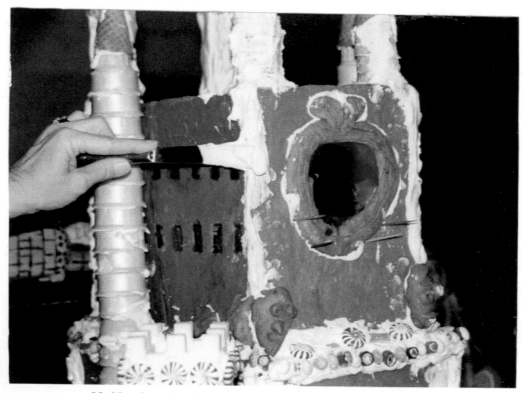

*My Mom is putting icing on the corners so that we can decorate.*

C over the spot that you are going to decorate with paste and then stick on the candy. Make sure that your area is not too big or the paste will dry before you put the candy on it. We also cover the ground with paste so that it looks like snow.

*We use nonpareils for the roof and walkways, candies that look like rocks to go around the base of the castle and to line the moat, blue rock candy for the water in the moat, ribbon candy to outline the roof, and peppermint sticks to go on the corners of the towers.*

# XI. The final product

**A**fter we are done decorating, we carefully move it from the kitchen to the dining room. Then we light it up every night of the holidays. This year the final product was a two-story gingerbread castle and it was the biggest that we have ever done.

*Here is the final product- our gingerbread castle for 1994.*

# XII. The smashing ceremony

E very year on my birthday, February 12, we smash our gingerbread castle with our neighborhood friends. Starting with the youngest and ending with the oldest, we use a hammer and take turns swinging at the castle. Each child gets a bag of gingerbread pieces to take home and eat. Then we look forward to making next year's castle!

*After the first round, the castle took a hard beating.*

*This is a model of Eugene Field School that we made with left-over gingerbread dough last year. My whole class, the "Renfro Combo", decorated it in the school library.*

# Gingerbread Gallery

1987

1988

1989

1992

# AFTERWORD

St. Basil's 1995

Notre Dame 1996

Taj Mahal 1997

Neighbor's House 1999

Sydney Opera House 2000

Imperial Hotel,
Chestertown, MD 2008

Ian (23 years) and Jonathan (27 years)
still making gingerbread

Made in the USA
Middletown, DE
12 October 2023

40700187R00018